Dismissing an Employee

Pocket Mentor Series

The *Pocket Mentor* Series offers immediate solutions to common challenges managers face on the job every day. Each book in the series is packed with handy tools, self-tests, and real-life examples to help you identify your strengths and weaknesses and hone critical skills. Whether you're at your desk, in a meeting, or on the road, these portable guides enable you to tackle the daily demands of your work with greater speed, savvy, and effectiveness.

Books in the series:

Leading Teams

Running Meetings

Managing Time

Managing Projects

Coaching People

Giving Feedback

Leading People

Negotiating Outcomes

Writing for Business

Giving Presentations

Understanding Finance

Dismissing an Employee

Dismissing an Employee

Expert Solutions to Everyday Challenges

Harvard Business School Publishing

Boston, Massachusetts

Copyright 2007 Harvard Business School Publishing Corporation

Printed in the United States of America

11 10 09 08 07   5 4 3 2 1

Library of Congress Cataloging-in-Publication Data

Dismissing an employee : expert solutions to everyday challenges.
    p. cm. — (Pocket mentor series)
  Includes bibliographical references.
  ISBN-13: 978-1-4221-1884-9 (pbk. : alk. paper)
  1. Employees—Dismissal of. 2. Employees—Dismissal of—Law and
legislation. I. Harvard Business School Publishing Corporation.
  HF5549.5.D55D584 2007
  658.3'13—dc22

                                    2007019483

The paper used in this publication meets the requirements of the American National
Standard for Permanence of Paper for Publications and Documents in Libraries and
Archives Z39.48-1992

Contents

Handling a Dismissal Professionally 31

Strategies for conducting a dismissal meeting.

Handling the Legal Details After a Dismissal 41

Suggestions for dealing with important legal concerns.

Leading Your Team After a Dismissal 49

Ways to ensure that your team keeps functioning at top form.

Learning from a Dismissal   53

Strategies for improving your handling of dismissals.

Furthering your personal and professional growth   54

Gaining a broader view   55

Identifying ways to improve   56

Preserving your organization's integrity   56

Tips and Tools   57

Tools for Dismissing an Employee   59

Worksheets you can use to effectively handle dismissals.

Test Yourself   63

A helpful review of concepts presented in this guide. Take it before and after you've read the guide to see how much you've learned.

Answers to test questions   66

Frequently Asked Questions   69

Look here for answers and practical advice on overcoming typical dismissal problems.

Key Terms   73

Read this list to learn the meaning of important terms.

Mentors' Message: Handling a Dismissal Skillfully

For many managers, dismissing an employee is the most difficult and painful decision they must face. Emotions run high. A manager wonders how he or she could have prevented this uncomfortable outcome and what the legal ramifications might be. The manager also wonders how colleagues of the dismissed employee will react and who will handle the workload afterward. In addition, managers often worry whether the dismissal had anything to do with their own performance or behavior.

But despite the intense discomfort that comes with dismissing an employee, it's vital that you handle this task correctly. A poorly conducted dismissal can carry immense costs. For one thing, it can hurt your company's reputation—making it harder for you and other managers to attract and retain talented employees in the future. It can also lead to lawsuits as well as destroy trust and morale among employees throughout the organization.

For these reasons, you need to take steps to ensure that you handle a dismissal professionally and correctly. That means gaining familiarity with every aspect of dismissing an employee—from how to make the decision and prepare for the dismissal meeting to what to say during the meeting and how to lead your team afterward.

Dismissing an employee will never be easy, and each dismissal offers important learning opportunities. But by applying the practices suggested in this guide—and by always relying on advice from your company's human resources and legal experts—you boost your chances of obtaining the best possible outcome. When you handle a dismissal skillfully, you safeguard your firm's reputation, enable your team to move forward despite the pain of the situation, and protect your company from legal liability—all crucial results for any organization seeking to succeed in a challenging marketplace.

Susan Alvey, Mentor

Dr. Alvey is an organizational and leadership development consultant in Cambridge, Massachusetts. She works closely with executives to ensure their people strategy supports their business strategy and aligns structures, roles, and incentives to optimize organizational functioning. She previously led learning and organizational development at Harvard Business School Publishing and currently teaches in the MBA program at Babson College.

Steven Robbins, Mentor

Steven Robbins is a veteran of nine high-growth start-ups and three IPOs over the last thirty years. He was on the design team of Harvard Business School's (HBS's) Leadership and Learning curriculum redesign, and currently advises and coaches executives in several industries, including financial services, high-tech, and health care. Steven has had columns on Entrepreneur.com and HBS Working Knowledge, and has appeared widely on radio, on television, and in print.

Dismissing an Employee: The Basics

A Difficult
Moment

WHILE NO ONE LIKES to be the bearer of bad news, managers are sometimes faced with the difficult task of having to dismiss an employee whose performance just can't be brought up to par.

This can be one of the most difficult and painful tasks in any manager's life. In fact, the heightened emotions, serious legal implications, and other concerns associated with dismissing an employee can be so complex and intense that many managers avoid even discussing them.

Why learn about dismissals?

Unfortunately, dismissing employees is a fact of organizational life. Managers who shy away from learning about dismissals risk handling the situation badly. And a poorly handled dismissal can:

- Permanently damage managers' reputations and professional self-esteem
- Corrode a company's reputation in its industry, making it harder for the company to attract and retain talented employees
- Lead to lawsuits
- Destroy trust and morale within the organization
- Prompt high performers who know they're very marketable to leave the company

The more you know about dismissing employees, the better prepared you'll be to handle the situation if it arises.

Defining the term

To *dismiss* an employee is to terminate an individual's employment with a company owing to inadequacies or problems with his or her performance or behavior.

The table "Dismissal attributes" summarizes the main attributes of dismissals.

DISMISS *v* **1:** to terminate an individual's employment with a company owing to inadequacies or problems with his or her performance or behavior

---

Dismissal attributes

Reason	Based on an employee's problematic performance or behavior
Decision maker	You, the manager, decide and implement
Emotions	Mostly relief for managers; negative emotions for the dismissed employee
Legal issues	Managers must let the company's legal department guide them through the process
Effectiveness	Will usually solve the problem at hand—unless the manager has a history of unnecessary dismissals

A note about dismissal terminology

Organizations use different terms for dismissing an employee. Examples include *firing*, *terminating*, *letting go*, *sacking*, and *discharging*. Often one company avoids a term used by another. In addition, some terms do not cross cultures meaningfully. For these reasons, we have chosen to use the generic term *dismissal* throughout this topic.

DISCLAIMER: At several points, this topic refers to legal concerns involved in making and communicating the decision to dismiss an employee. It is not intended as legal advice. You should consult with legal counsel who can advise you on the specifics of your situation.

A Closer Look at Dismissals

> *Sooner or later, every conscientious*
> *person who owns or manages a*
> *business for an appreciable*
> *time will need to do the same hard*
> *thing: fire someone.*
> —Barbara Kate Repa

When do dismissals occur?

Dismissals occur whenever a manager decides that an employee's performance or behavior is hopelessly problematic. In some cases, an employee outright violates a law or a company policy (for example, by stealing or by sexually harassing another employee) and is dismissed immediately. In other cases, the manager has worked with the employee over many months to try to address performance or behavioral problems, but these efforts have not succeeded. In general, you, the manager, would decide whether to dismiss an employee. You would also be the one to deliver the news.

What emotions are associated with dismissals?

For most managers, dismissing a problem employee generates a feeling of relief. That's because dismissing usually solves the problem at hand. However, some managers may feel a sense of failure because they see themselves as responsible for being unable to improve matters. For employees who are dismissed, feelings can range from anger, sadness, and resignation to shame, frustration, rage, or even relief—depending on the individual involved and the circumstances surrounding the dismissal.

Workers who remain may experience strong emotions as well, depending on their relationship with the dismissed employee. Friends and supporters of the former team member may feel angry. Those who felt frustrated by the dismissed person's poor performance may feel relieved.

What are the legal implications of dismissals?

Dismissals can happen in any organization and in any industry. However, dismissal regulations vary widely internationally. Laws and company policies governing dismissals are complex. Various forms of employee status—such as exempt versus nonexempt or union versus nonunion—add to this complexity. A general awareness of these implications can help guide you when dismissing an employee.

Tip: *Always* follow your firm's dismissal-related policies exactly and seek legal advice from your internal or external corporate counsel. Sloppy handling of a dismissal can result in a wrongful-dismissal suit, so let your company's legal department guide you every step of the way.

How effectively do dismissals solve the problem?

Dismissals usually solve the problem at hand—whether it's poor performance on the employee's part or problematic behavior that severely disrupts team performance. However, sometimes dismissals stem *in part* from a manager's failure to give timely and sufficient feedback and support to the problem employee.

Tip: Take the time to learn from a dismissal—to identify what (if anything) you could have done better to help the employee improve. If you don't do this, a pattern of unnecessary dismissals may emerge in your team or department.

Taking Care of
Yourself During a
Dismissal

DECIDING WHETHER TO dismiss an employee puts significant emotional strain on any manager—no matter how experienced he or she is. By acknowledging the difficult aspects of this event, you can more effectively manage your emotions and stress level.

Acknowledging the emotional impact

During the decision process, you may experience one or more of the following feelings:

- **Anxiety** over whether dismissing the employee is the right decision—should you do something more to try to solve the person's performance or behavior problem?

- **Sadness** over the possibility of losing an employee who may have positive personal qualities and who may be your friend

- **A sense of failure** because you can't find a more positive solution to the problem

- **Concern** over whether the affected employee will suffer severe financial hardship if dismissed

- **Fear** that a dismissed employee may seek retribution or take legal action against the company

- **Relief** that you'll finally be rid of a chronic problem employee

> **Tip:** Consider using a communications coach to provide emotional support during dismissals. A good communications coach can help you sort through the emotional complexities that often characterize such situations. He or she can also help you maintain needed perspective and can replenish your energy just by listening.

Acknowledging the uncertainty

You may also feel some confusion or uncertainty over how to decide whether to dismiss a worker or how to actually implement a dismissal if matters should come to that. For example, you may be wondering:

- When it's legal to dismiss someone
- Whether you have enough evidence to make the decision
- How and when to communicate with an affected employee
- How to handle the dismissal according to legal and company policy
- How to preserve morale and trust among remaining team members who may question the dismissal decision or who may have been friends with the affected employee
- How to realign work roles, systems, and processes in your team or department after the person leaves so that his or her former responsibilities are handled effectively

What Would YOU Do?

Marshalling Courage for a Tough Decision

WHEN KIA HIRED Marshall, she had been impressed with his energy and drive. He was enthusiastic and learned their products quickly. A few months later, Kia sat looking at Marshall's sales reports. He wasn't meeting his goals—in fact, he wasn't even coming close. Everyone in the department was hitting their revenue targets except for him. In addition, his reports were disorganized and incomplete. Some were even missing!

Kia shook her head sadly. How could she have been so wrong? Marshall might have the personality for sales, but he sure lacked the discipline and organizational skills to be truly successful. Maybe it was time to cut her losses and let Marshall go. What other choice did she have?

Managing yourself

It's vital that you find ways to take care of *yourself* during this difficult time. Only then can you put yourself in the best possible position to handle the dismissal effectively. Begin with these steps:

- **Understand** that dismissing someone may have difficult consequences for everyone—you, the affected employee, and your remaining team members. Once implemented, a dismissal can be difficult even for people *outside* the company. For example, a customer or supplier who had established a professional connection with the affected employee may wonder why he or she has been dismissed or question the performance of the entire team.

- **Acknowledge** that if you've truly tried everything to help solve the employee's performance or behavior problem, you've done your best to give him or her a fair chance to improve. Realize, too, that being dismissed may actually be a relief for the affected employee. After all, few people enjoy being in a job where things aren't working out.

- **Discuss** your feelings about the situation with your support network outside of your organization—your family members, friends, colleagues, and others who are good listeners—and ask them how they might handle the emotions associated with the decision.

What You COULD Do.

Let's go back to Kia's dilemma.

The mentors suggest this solution:

While dismissing an employee may seem like the only solution to a problem, there are other alternatives worth exploring. For example, Kia might consider coaching Marshall to clarify performance expectations. She might also consider sending him to a training session to improve his sales skills. If the situation doesn't improve, she might then decide to issue Marshall a formal warning or put him on probation. It's important for Kia to document Marshall's poor performance and note the steps she's taken to help him improve. Throughout the process, Kia should consult her human resource department and/or legal counsel to ensure that she's following her company's policies and procedures correctly.

Understanding the Grounds for a Dismissal

HOW DO YOU DETERMINE whether you can legally dismiss an employee? It's crucial to familiarize yourself with the grounds for a dismissal as well as the conditions under which you cannot legally dismiss an employee.

When you can dismiss an employee immediately

In the United States, offenses for which immediate dismissal is almost always justifiable include:

- Possessing an unapproved weapon at work

- Flagrantly violating the most serious company rules; for example, giving away trade secrets to competitors

- Being dishonest about significant workplace issues; for instance, lying about one's expenses or sales

- Endangering coworkers' health and safety

- Sexually harassing coworkers or otherwise threatening them in ways that prevent them from doing their work

- Engaging in criminal activity

- Using alcohol or drugs at work

- Gambling on the job

Laws vary from state to state and from nation to nation. Consult internal or external legal counsel to make sure you understand the regulations unique to your situation.

When to proceed with documentation

In U.S. businesses, the following workplace wrongs merit dismissal if they persist or go uncorrected after you bring them to the employee's attention:

- Performing poorly on the job

- Refusing to follow instructions

- Having a persistent negative or destructive attitude

- Being insubordinate

- Abusing sick leave and other privileges

- Being chronically late or absent

No matter which country you work in, once again, consult internal or external counsel to make sure you understand the regulations or policies unique to your situation.

There are many reasons, beyond the above, why a manager might dismiss an employee. Whatever your reason for dismissal, it's vital to document the employee's behavior and the steps you've taken to correct it. Being able to point to a history of problem behavior in documented employee performance reviews, personnel-file memos, and private notes can be invaluable if a dismissed employee claims that his or her dismissal was unjustified.

When you cannot dismiss an employee

In many countries, there are certain behaviors for which a company cannot legally dismiss an employee. These vary nation by nation, but examples may include employee behaviors such as:

- Filing a workers' compensation claim

- "Blowing the whistle" on illegal behavior on the company's part

- Reporting or complaining about company violations of occupational safety and health laws

- Exercising the right to belong or not to belong to a union

- Taking time off from work to perform a civic duty, such as serve on a jury or vote

- Taking a day off from work that was available under federal or state law

Again, ask your internal or external counsel to advise you regarding these regulations. Note that some laws—such as those pertaining to occupational health and safety—can vary state by state or from country to country. The key point? The rules are complicated. Familiarize yourself with them—but don't try to interpret them on your own.

A special note about discrimination

Various countries have established federal- and state-level laws against dismissing employees based on their:

- Race

- Gender

- Sexual orientation

- Marital status

- Physical or mental disability

- Age

- Reproductive status (that is, whether they're pregnant or plan to become pregnant)

Laws and the court decisions that interpret them can be tricky to apply to particular situations. However, it's essential that you pay scrupulous attention to how employment discrimination is defined in your situation before deciding whether to dismiss someone. That's because discrimination is the most often cited reason for wrongful-discharge claims, and employment discrimination laws are complicated and can change quickly.

Familiarizing yourself with company procedures

Whether you work for a large or small company or head your own firm, a carelessly handled dismissal can result in wrongful-dismissal or discrimination lawsuits. Thus you'll need to pay close attention to federal and state laws, and industry policies governing dismissal decisions and implementation.

If you work in a large company, thoroughly familiarize yourself with your company's established procedures for dismissing an employee (including how to document problem performance or behavior, what to say to the affected employee, when to say it, and so forth). Learn about applicable federal, state, or employment-status regulations as well (such as laws regarding dismissal of exempt versus nonexempt personnel or union versus nonunion employees).

The human resource and legal departments will have clear policies and procedures in place regarding dismissing an employee. Your supervisor may also provide you with helpful documents—which may even include a script specifying exactly what to say when you break the news to the affected employee.

Whatever the case, be sure to follow these procedures carefully to avoid a mishandled dismissal. Let your company's legal counsel guide you step-by-step through the process.

If you work in a small company that lacks human resource and legal departments, the firm's upper management may have consulted external counsel for guidance on dismissal decisions and implementation. Follow counsel's instructions precisely.

If you own a small entrepreneurial firm and don't have an attorney on staff, consult external legal counsel regarding dismissal laws and procedures and follow his or her advice. If you do have an attorney on staff, follow his or her guidance every step of the way.

CAUTION: Employment law is a specialized field. Be sure that the attorney advising you is an experienced practitioner in this area.

Making
the Decision

W HEN DO YOU DECIDE that it's time to dismiss an employee? In some cases, you may be justified in dismissing a worker immediately—for example, if he or she steals from the company or abuses company confidentiality. However, in cases of poor work performance or behavior problems that stop short of being illegal, experts suggest using a dismissal as a last resort. The following guidelines can help you make the right decision.

Proceeding with caution

It's best to proceed with caution when you're considering dismissing an employee. That's because replacing dismissed employees can get expensive, after you've totaled up advertising, recruiting, screening, and hiring costs. Indeed, some analysts say that replacing a dismissed employee can end up costing roughly *twice* the salary that the position pays.

Dismissals can also create unease and resentment among remaining team members who question the rationale behind the decision or who consider the dismissed employee their friend. In addition, they can carry the risk of legal action from the affected employee. Even if the company handled the dismissal in a perfectly legal manner, responding to a lawsuit can sap a company's energy and financial resources.

Exploring alternatives to dismissals

In light of the risks and costs involved in dismissing an employee, it's worth exploring alternatives to dismissals if they apply. Alternatives include:

- **Training** designed to strengthen the employee's skills

- **Counseling or coaching** to clarify performance or behavior expectations and pinpoint areas for improvement

- **Reassigning** the employee to a position that provides a better match between his or her talents and the company's or department's needs

- **Warnings** that increase in severity and that get documented in the employee's personnel file

- **Putting the employee on probation;** that is, temporarily suspending some workplace benefits (such as flextime or the opportunity to work from home) until the employee improves his or her performance or behavior

- **Suspending the employee,** giving him or her time off (paid or unpaid) to formulate a revised work plan or set new goals

- **Postponing a pay raise** until the employee shows improvement

- **Demoting the employee** to a position with fewer responsibilities and less pay

Selecting alternatives

To select from among these alternatives, decide whether the employee's problem stems primarily from inadequate performance or inappropriate behavior.

Inadequate performance includes problems such as missed production targets, consistently botched client presentations, and so forth. In this case, you'd be more likely to try alternatives such as training or reassignment.

Inappropriate behavior may take the form of destructive gossiping, chronic blaming of others, a negative or listless demeanor, inappropriate humor, or chronic lateness and constantly missed deadlines. In this case, you'd be more likely to try alternatives such as counseling or coaching (see the table "Coaching problem employees").

In considering inappropriate behavior, focus on conduct that is clearly disruptive to team goals and productivity (not merely annoying to a few of the employee's colleagues) or has a demonstrable impact on other employees.

Coaching problem employees

Problematic behavior doesn't automatically have to lead to a dismissal of an employee. Try coaching first with these problem-employee "breeds."

Breed	Coaching strategy
Gossipmongers	Warn the person that gossip and inflammatory rumors can hurt the whole organization. Work to redirect a gossipmonger's energy in more positive ways. If necessary, consider relocating this individual so you can monitor his or her productivity more easily.
Blamers	Point out that chronic blaming of others for things that go wrong hurts the team *and* the company. Consider shuffling workloads around to better balance the tasks at hand. Watch to see whether your changes solve the problem. If not, take steps toward a performance improvement plan or employment termination.
Downers	Tell the person that a constant negative attitude can be highly damaging to a team's enthusiasm and commitment. Show concern that the person isn't happy on the job. Listen to and deal with specific complaints. Solicit suggestions for improving the way your team works.
Know-it-alls	Explain that employees who constantly brag about their superior abilities can wear down a team's spirit. Acknowledge the person's positive attributes or skills while also encouraging him or her to respect and value other employees' capabilities.
Slackers	Point out that low productivity due to repeated absences or tardiness, frequent disorganization, or inability to set priorities frustrates other team members and makes them become angry and resentful. If poor performance stems from personal problems, consider adjusting the person's work schedule to ease the burden. If it's due to pure laziness, take steps toward a performance improvement plan or employment termination.
Jokesters	Tell the person that racist, homophobic, sexist, or offensive comments are unacceptable in the workplace and that employees who persist in making these comments or jokes risk harassment complaints.

Handling a
Dismissal
Professionally

Those 15 minutes determine whether the employee sues you, poisons coworkers against you, or resorts to violence.

—Amy Delpo and Lisa Guerin

A T SOME POINT IN your career, you may have to dismiss an employee. Preparing and knowing what to say during the meeting can help you handle the situation professionally.

Preparing for a dismissal meeting

First, make sure you've done all the background work: Have you documented the employee's performance or behavior problems and the steps you've taken to help him or her improve? Have you consulted your company's legal and human resource departments regarding the dismissal regulations unique to your situation? Have you processed the difficult emotions associated with this decision?

You want to feel confident that dismissing the person is the right thing to do—for him or her, for your team, and for your company. The *really* tough part of the dismissal could be breaking the news to the affected employee. However, if you have done a good job of providing performance feedback to the employee, the dismissal should not come as a complete surprise. Still, unfortunately, some companies have suffered severe repercussions after

Seven Steps to Documenting Employee Performance Problems

1. Consider using all forms of documentation—annual performance reviews, improvement plans, disciplinary steps, written warnings, personal notes, memos, and e-mails.
2. Make sure your documents contain nothing that you wouldn't discuss with the employee.
3. Concentrate on objective work-performance issues, not personal criticism.
4. Reflect cool, reasoned observations.
5. Make sure all documents are dated and hard copies are signed.
6. Store records digitally, and keep copies of printed materials.
7. File all records in a confidential, secure place.

dismissing someone. A dismissed employee may deliver an angry or destructive outburst or inflict threatening letters or phone calls on the company. He or she might also sabotage company assets or launch (or threaten) a wrongful-dismissal lawsuit.

By handling the dismissal thoughtfully, you can do your best to ensure that none of these things happen. Certainly, there is no easy way to implement a dismissal. However, you can mitigate the amount of pain the affected employee will experience and protect your company from legal or other kinds of retribution by being careful about *when*, *where*, and *how* you dismiss an employee, and about *what* you say during this critical discussion.

When to schedule the meeting

Some experts advise against dismissing an employee on a Friday afternoon. A dismissal notice just before a weekend *may* cause the person to stew over the weekend and possibly ponder a lawsuit or think about returning to the office with disruptive intentions.

Consider scheduling a meeting on a Monday afternoon. That way, he or she has all week to start looking for another job, and you'll minimize the impact of the dismissal notice on other employees.

Under some circumstances, you may want to allow time for good-byes. However, don't let the dismissed employee mix with other workers for too long unless you can trust that he or she is not going to express extreme criticism of the action to other employees. If you do allow good-byes, identify whom the employee is allowed to meet with and for how long.

Where to hold the meeting

Meet with the employee in a place that keeps both of you out of plain sight, such as a windowless conference room or office, or some other space that gives you complete privacy. Also, arrange for a path to and from the meeting to avoid areas that are likely to be populated by curious coworkers.

Why so much secrecy? Keeping the meeting private shows basic respect for the affected employee. No one wants to know that his or her coworkers are overhearing or seeing what may feel like a humiliating experience.

Also, if other employees witness or overhear what's going on, they may develop a "siege mentality." That is, without much more information than glum or tense faces or voices, they may worry that they're one misstep away from being dismissed themselves or feel protective toward the affected employee (especially if they consider him or her a friend).

SIEGE MENTALITY *n* **1:** the common feeling among colleagues of a dismissed employee that they are about to be dismissed themselves

---

How to handle the meeting

To handle the dismissal as effectively as possible, don't go it alone. Always make sure someone from human resources is present at the meeting. He or she can:

- Serve as an impassive voice if you or the employee becomes overly emotional during the meeting

- Answer the inevitable questions regarding pensions, insurance, and severance pay

- Suggest ways the employee can tell his or her spouse or partner about the dismissal

- Act as a buffer in case of an emotional or physical outburst from the employee

- Serve as a witness to the conversation in case a dispute emerges later about what you said

Also, get the meeting over with as quickly as possible. The more concisely you convey the news to the employee, the less prone you'll be to say something that might expose your company to liability. Keep the meeting to five minutes—ten minutes at the most.

In addition, remember to be dispassionate, direct, and focused. Convey a sense of serious purpose and resoluteness. To avoid planting the seeds for legal problems later, resist the temptation to apologize or to reconsider your decision in light of protests from the employee. Don't try to sugarcoat your message or give the impression that your decision can be negotiated. Instead, be as unemotional and resolute as possible.

Tip: Make sure the person knows that your decision to dismiss him or her is final. Don't give the impression that the decision is open to negotiation.

What to say—and not say—during the meeting

The words and tone of voice you use in a dismissal meeting are crucial. Strive to apply the following practices:

- Explain in general terms that the job has not worked out. If you choose to explain in more detail, do so in an objective, neutral tone that doesn't make the employee feel personally attacked.

  Examples might include the following: "We talked about your not meeting the performance goals for your role six months ago. You still haven't met them." "You've received coaching and counseling to work on your critical attitude toward colleagues, but your behavior hasn't changed."

Tip: Practice speaking in a neutral voice, so you can convey neutrality during a dismissal meeting. Voice tone conveys emotion heavily. Practice intonations and listen carefully for sarcasm, distress, or any highly emotional message your voice may be sending. Practicing into a tape recorder can help.

By citing objective reasons in a neutral tone, you'll lessen the chances that the person will sue or bad-mouth you or the company—something that can come back to haunt you during acute labor shortages.

- **Strike a balance between being concise and direct, and being empathetic.** That is, do acknowledge that losing a job is likely to have a profound impact on the person's life; for example, "I know this is hard for you." After delivering the news, give the person time to vent his or her anger, confusion, or bitterness for a few moments. Empathy and a chance to process emotions can help people bear difficult news.

- **Deliver the news in a way that preserves the person's dignity.** This includes making arrangements for the employee to remove his or her personal effects from the office during off-hours or over the weekend (with monitoring from someone in the company). Employees who are made to feel humiliated before colleagues or disrespected and personally attacked during a dismissal will be more likely to feel angry and thus desire retribution.

- **If severance is offered, consider offering as generous a package as possible.** A generous severance package can help to salve any concerns about future security that the employee may feel. (You'll need to consult with your boss to see what kinds of package budgets might allow.)

As for what *not* to say during a dismissal, remember that the specific language you use while dismissing an employee can play a major role in whether the person decides to sue. Therefore, language merits a focused discussion here. Use the following "don'ts" as guidelines during a dismissal:

- Don't side with the worker or foster an "us against them" mind-set to ease your own discomfort. For example, don't say, "Personally, I don't think that letting you go is the right decision."

- Don't tell a dismissed employee that the dismissal is part of a layoff. This "white lie" could come back to haunt you in the form of a discrimination suit if you hire someone new to fill the vacated position—and the former employee finds out about it through his or her ex-coworkers.

- Don't say anything like, "We're after a more dynamic, aggressive workforce," "You just don't fit into the team," "We need people with fewer family commitments who can see clients after normal work hours," or "We need to project a high-energy image." These kinds of statements could give the impression that the employee is being dismissed for discriminatory reasons, such as being too old, foreign, married, and so forth.

- Don't use humor or try to make light of the situation. You'll only make the meeting even more painfully awkward. Worse, you may make the person feel laughed at or humiliated—and therefore more motivated to sue for wrongful dismissal.

- Don't threaten an employee who implies that he or she may challenge the dismissal; for example, by implying that you'll withhold the person's final paycheck unless he or she agrees not to sue. These forms of persuasion are considered illegal coercion and would come back to haunt you in court.

Tip: If you need practice handling a dismissal meeting, consider getting help from a communications coach. With your coach, work on skills such as communicating difficult news in a timely manner, tailoring your delivery style to the demands of the situation, avoiding unclear or inflammatory language, listening to employees' concerns and emotions, and conveying empathy and resolve simultaneously.

Learning from the dismissal meeting

No matter how difficult a dismissal meeting may be, it may yield information that can help you make important improvements in your group. But to gain that information, you'll need to provide opportunities for the dismissed employee to communicate his or her opinions, and then listen to them objectively.

For example, if the employee has numerous thoughts about what went wrong, encourage him or her to write them down in a letter or memo and to share them during an exit interview. With nothing at stake any longer, the former employee may offer candid opinions of oppressive policies or other problems that you can use later to identify and implement needed changes. At the very least, by making the individual feel that his or her views are important enough to take seriously, you'll help ease the pain of the situation and shore up the person's self-esteem.

Also, be sure to listen as well as talk during the dismissal meeting. A person who is being dismissed may speak more openly about workplace problems than other employees will. By reviewing parting comments (even if they're barbs) objectively, you may be able to identify weaknesses in your group that you can correct. Still, during the dismissal meeting, do not make any promises to change the way you manage your group.

Handling the Legal Details After a Dismissal

T HERE ARE NUMEROUS legal details to attend to after you've dismissed an employee. By understanding these details, you can ensure that you've handled each one properly.

Reviewing the employment contract

One risk in dismissing an employee is that he or she will use the knowledge and contacts gained at your firm to start a competing business or work for a competitor. To protect themselves from these possibilities, many companies ask workers to sign noncompete and nondisclosure agreements.

In some areas, the law also requires employers to provide dismissed workers with what are called *service letters*, which describe their work histories and explain the reason for their dismissal.

And union members may have a collective-bargaining agreement that may specify terms or processes for termination of their employment with the company.

With all such agreements, you should discuss the terms of the document face-to-face with the affected employee, either during the employment-termination conversation or immediately afterward.

Through noncompete agreements, former employees promise not to work for a direct competitor for a specific length of time. Some companies ask employees to sign noncompete agreements upon hiring; others do so upon termination of employment. Your firm may have a hard time enforcing such an agreement if the covenant:

- Specifies too lengthy a time period

- Covers too wide a geographic area

- Is overly broad in the types of business it prohibits

The terms of noncompete agreements vary from country to country and industry to industry, and can change even within countries and industries whenever workplace realities change. For example, in the United States, many noncompete agreements used to specify a two-year period during which a dismissed employee could not compete directly against his or her former firm. That period has shortened considerably as companies realize that two years away from a particular job may make a worker stale and unemployable, and that the information an employee carries away from a company loses its value over a shorter period. Check with your company's human resource and legal departments to see what they recommend.

Through nondisclosure agreements, dismissed employees promise not to use sensitive information about your company to their advantage. Again, your company may ask employees to sign such a document upon hiring or upon termination of employment. Sensitive information may include trade secrets that give your company a competitive advantage, such as a chemical formula, special technique, recipe, or software program. It may also include customer lists, plans to sell the company, or insider knowledge about a company's plans to go public.

What Would YOU Do?

Sad News

PAUL SAT AT HIS desk with his head in his hands. He had just dismissed Tina for intractable performance problems, and he knew he had to deliver the news to the rest of his team. He was well aware that many of his employees had forged close friendships with Tina and would be sad to see her go. He dreaded having to tell them what had happened.

Trying to identify the best way to approach the task, he reviewed his options. Maybe he could send an e-mail to his subordinates explaining the situation. Or would it be better to meet face-to-face with each of them one at a time? What about calling the team together and giving them the news all at once?

Wrung out emotionally after the dismissal meeting, Paul felt overwhelmed by the many different possibilities for communicating the dismissal to his team.

Such agreements can vary widely in the kind of information covered and the length of time during which the dismissed employee must agree not to share the information. As with non-compete agreements, consult your human resource and legal departments for guidance.

Service letters also vary widely depending on where your company is operating. In the United States, for example, each state has different laws regarding whether employers must provide service letters to former employees.

Tip: Ask your firm's human resource and legal departments whether the company must provide a service letter for dismissed employees and, if so, what topics it must cover. If a service letter is required, you may need to provide specific information about the former employee's work history and performance or behavior problems.

Finally, collective-bargaining agreements apply when you need to dismiss a union member. As with the other kinds of agreements, consult your human resource and legal departments to make sure that you are honoring any employment-termination processes or terms stipulated in a collective-bargaining agreement.

Documenting the terms of the dismissal

After you've dismissed an employee, it's a good idea to document all the details pertaining to the end of the relationship. You or your company's human resource department can do this through what's called a separation letter addressed to the employee and delivered to him or her during an exit interview. The letter should clarify when the worker's employment ended. Depending on the circumstances of the situation, it may contain additional information as well (see "Your separation-letter checklist").

If the dismissed employee is in what's known as a protected class—such as a minority, disabled, female, or older worker—*and* he or she has agreed to sign a release, laws regarding the acceptance of the separation letter become more complicated. In this case, you or your company should consult legal counsel regarding exactly how to word the separation letter.

Avoiding damage to the person's reputation

Once the dismissed employee has left the company, take care not to do or say anything that anyone could perceive as damaging to

---

DISSMISSING AN EMPLOYEE

Your separation-letter checklist

Use this checklist to make sure you've included all pertinent information in a separation letter to a dismissed employee.

- ☐ Date the worker's employment ended
- ☐ Severance benefits, if any, including what kinds and when they will be provided
- ☐ Final pay, including any bonuses due and accrued benefits, such as vacation time
- ☐ Health-insurance coverage or conversion (for example, COBRA in the United States)
- ☐ Outplacement help
- ☐ Treatment of vested stock options
- ☐ Any noncompete or nondisclosure agreements
- ☐ Any terms stipulated in a collective-bargaining agreement
- ☐ Any agreements you've made about providing the person with a service letter or references
- ☐ Any release the worker has agreed to—that is, a promise not to sue the company in exchange for special benefits, such as additional money

---

the former employee's reputation or chances of finding another job. Perceived damaging comments can take the shape of informal statements you make to other people about the former employee or more formal references you give as the person begins interviewing with other employers.

Uttering something damning about a former worker—even if it's true or offered in the most casual setting—can have several negative consequences. Specifically, the dismissed employee may find out about your comment and bring defamation charges against you or your company. In addition, your remaining team members may perceive your behavior as callous and begin questioning how much you care about *them*.

In particular, beware of saying anything that implies that the dismissed person committed a crime, was incompetent at his or her job, abused drugs or alcohol, or acted in some other way that suggests he or she is unfit for a particular job. These statements become problematic if the former employee sues your company for wrongful discharge or defamation. Moreover, some information is not legally permissible to reveal—such as the fact that a former employee has an arrest record. The best policy is simply not to say anything negative about a former employee.

If the former employee asks you for a reference and you feel you have little or nothing good to say about the person, stick to the bare essentials. Indeed, your company may have a clear policy specifying what information you can provide in a reference. Check with your human resource and legal departments to familiarize yourself with your company's references policies.

What You COULD Do.

Remember Paul's dilemma—how to tell his team he had just dismissed Tina?

The mentors suggest this solution:

Paul should hold a team meeting and announce to his group that Tina has been dismissed. After making the announcement, he needs to invite team members to raise concerns and questions. In particular, to combat siege mentality, he should be sure to let them know that Tina's dismissal had nothing to do with their own on-the-job performance. During the meeting, he should also acknowledge that dismissals are difficult for everyone. After the meeting, Paul might also meet with team members individually. That way, they can voice any concerns that they didn't feel comfortable expressing in the group meeting.

Tip: Watch out for disgruntled former employees who may try to trap you into giving a negative reference—which they could then use against you. Before giving a reference, make sure the request comes from a legitimate source.

Leading Your Team After a Dismissal

If firing someone is hard for you,
imagine how your other employees will feel.
—Amy Delpo and Lisa Guerin

Y OUR WORK ISN'T finished just because you've dismissed an employee. You now need to take special steps to continue leading your team after the employee has departed. Communicating the dismissal and redistributing the workload are two especially important tasks.

Communicating the dismissal

Notify workers as soon as possible after someone has been dismissed. Pretending that nothing has happened will only fuel gossip or concerns among remaining group members that they'll be dismissed next. The best way to do this is to hold a team meeting in which you:

- Concisely explain what has happened. For example, you might say, "Elsa was dismissed yesterday because of chronic lateness" or "Toby was dismissed after many months of unsuccessful effort to improve his work performance." Do not go into detail or elaborate on your decision. Also, be sure not to criticize the former employee.

- Reassure team members that the dismissal had nothing to do with their own performance or behavior.

- Acknowledge that this is a difficult time for the entire department and that you understand people will be feeling uncomfortable about it.

- Explain what your plans are for seeking a replacement and whether the team's focus will change because of the employee's departure.

After the meeting, schedule time with each person to listen to his or her concerns and help them process their feelings about the change. Ask what you can do to help people navigate through this difficult time.

Redistributing work

After you've dismissed an employee, talk with your team about how best to redistribute the workload. Reassign projects and tasks in a way that's realistic, fair, and manageable for the remaining team members and that enables them to remain productive and positive.

Equally important, you'll need to decide what to do about the former employee's formal *and* informal skills. If you aren't planning to replace the former employee, or if you think it will take a while to recruit someone new, you'll need to ensure that the dismissed employee's skills are covered by other individuals in the group.

For example, a former employee may have had important social skills ("Ramon always knew how to smooth out disagreements") or technical skills ("Talia was the only one who knew how to use that graphics software"). In either case, other team members will need to take responsibility for ensuring that those skills are still present in the group.

Talk about these skill gaps with your team, and work out ways to get them covered by the most appropriate individuals. Your team may feel understandably hesitant to offer ideas or ask for changes, so you will need to clarify how these decisions will be made.

Tip: To fill gaps in formal technical skills that a dismissed employee had, you may need to provide training for certain employees. With social-dynamic skills, consider simply inviting people to take responsibility for representing those skills in the group.

Learning from a
Dismissal

I survived the experience—and learned
how to do it better next time.

—A manager

A S HARD AND upsetting as dismissing an employee is, it offers numerous important learning opportunities. As with any new and difficult experience, it's valuable to spend some time afterward assessing what you've learned and achieved.

Furthering your personal and professional growth

Dismissing someone, though highly stressful, offers important opportunities for personal and professional growth. For example, you learn how to manage your own and others' emotions, how to master challenging new tasks, what your strengths as a manager are, and where you can improve your skills.

After making it through a dismissal, you may discover that you learned far more than you expected—and that you handled the situation more skillfully than you ever anticipated.

And if you feel dissatisfied with the way you dealt with any aspect of the process, you can objectively examine what went wrong and then use the resulting insights to do better next time.

In short, navigating through an employee dismissal gives you valuable new opportunities to enhance your knowledge, your managerial skills, and your personal and professional integrity.

Gaining a broader view

Dismissing employees teaches managers to broaden their view of this difficult, complex task in several ways. For one thing, you gain a new understanding of time horizon. Before experiencing a dismissal for the first time, many team leaders see the task from a narrow perspective; that is, they focus only on the moment in which the actual dismissal is implemented. But dismissing an employee has a much longer time horizon than that. You need to take important steps and make vital decisions before, during, and after the "main event."

For example, you need to identify when it's appropriate and legal to dismiss a problem worker, how to do so without incurring a lawsuit, and how to rebuild your team afterward. Thus the act of dismissing someone is just one narrow portion of the spectrum of decisions and actions the process entails.

You also gain a new view of "people horizon." You realize that you must not only manage the impact of a dismissal on directly affected employees; you must also manage the impact on the rest of your team.

PEOPLE HORIZON *n* **1:** the full range of individuals affected whenever an employee is dismissed

---

Identifying ways to improve

If you're dissatisfied with any aspect of your leadership before, during, and after a dismissal, you can learn from the experience and put better strategies and systems in place for next time.

Sometimes, dismissing employees stems from poor planning and ineffective performance management that occurred long before the employee dismissal.

Many experts maintain that "hiring smart" is *the* best way to avoid dismissals later. Hiring for attitude and social-dynamic ability as well as more formal skills can help you build a high-performing and stable team. And "strategic headcount planning" helps you expand and enrich your group wisely.

Preserving your organization's integrity

By skillfully implementing a dismissal, you also help preserve your organization's and team's integrity. That's because you sever a relationship between your company and an individual who simply is not contributing to the firm's success.

Though upsetting, dismissing a problem performer can help your team refocus on the work at hand. Indeed, many managers and teams feel relieved to finally say good-bye to an individual who has been draining the team's energy and spawning resentment or frustration throughout the group.

Handled skillfully, a dismissal can help you forge a stronger self, a stronger team, and a stronger company.

Tips and Tools

Tools for
Dismissing an Employee

List of Dos and Don'ts for Dismissing an Employee

Use this list as a quick reminder of what you should do or not do as part of the process of dismissing an employee. You can add to this list specific policies and practices within your company, as well as tips you've learned from experience.

Do ...	Don't ...
Do become familiar with your company's policies and procedures.	Don't tell a dismissed employee that the dismissal is part of a layoff if it isn't.
Do be informed about the legal implications of dismissing an employee. Be sure to seek legal advice from a knowledgeable attorney.	Don't use statements that could leave the impression that the employee is being dismissed for discriminatory reasons, such as being too old, married, pregnant, and so forth.
Do involve a human resource professional, if possible, in the plan and termination meeting.	Don't use humor or make light of the situation.
Do document the terms of the employee's dismissal and create a separation letter.	Don't threaten an employee who implies that he or she may challenge the dismissal.
Do acknowledge the emotional impact of this process on yourself and the employee.	Don't withhold the person's final paycheck.
Do be dispassionate, direct, and focused in the meeting, but deliver the message in a way that preserves the person's dignity.	Don't go it alone: have a human resource professional at the meeting, if possible.
Do keep the meeting short and private.	Don't make potentially damaging statements about the employee to fellow employees.
Do deliver a severance package, if possible, to ease employee concerns about security.	Don't make potentially damaging statements about the dismissed employee to his or her reference checks.
Do make arrangements for the employee to retrieve his or her personal belongings.	Don't apologize or reconsider your decision if the employee protests.
Do set up an exit interview, if possible.	Don't sugarcoat your message.
Do listen as well as talk; the employee may share more freely important information.	Don't make promises you can't keep.
Do honor employment contracts such as a union's collective-bargaining agreements, noncompete or nondisclosure agreements, or a service letter.	Don't just shut off the employee's e-mail and voice mail without careful decisions about what channels you want to keep open or closed.
Do concisely communicate to other workers appropriate information concerning the dismissal, including your plans for seeking a replacement.	
Do redistribute the dismissed employee's work, if necessary, in a way that enables others to remain productive.	
Do follow company policy regarding notifying external contacts.	

Additional Dos and Don'ts

Dismissal Preparation Checklist

Use this checklist to help you prepare for dismissing an employee. You can add company-specific procedures or your own personal items to this list.

Have You?	Yes	No
1. Determined that dismissal is now the best means of going forward for this employee, and that there are no other viable alternatives?		
2. Reviewed company policies and procedures on dismissing an employee?		
3. Sought legal advice on the soundness of your reasons and on how to manage the dismissal?		
4. Kept adequate records to document the employee's inadequate performance and measures taken to address it?		
5. Avoided making judgmental or discriminatory statements about the person that could end up being harmful to you or the company?		
6. Recognized and tried to deal with the emotional impact of making this decision on yourself and the other person?		
7. Sought appropriate support and guidance if this is your first dismissal?		
8. Thought through how you will present this situation to the employee and how you will handle difficult questions or behaviors?		
9. Asked a human resource professional, if possible or needed, to sit in on the dismissal session with you?		
10. Arranged a private place and reserved a time to have the conversation with the employee?		
11. Thought through how you will announce this dismissal to others in your work group?		
12. Made a plan to handle the dismissed employee's workload?		
13. Consulted with human resources about finding a replacement?		
14. Prepared all the necessary paperwork?		
15. Developed an exit plan for the employee that makes the dismissal day his or her last day and includes how e-mail or other communications will be handled internally or externally, how he or she can retrieve his or her belongings, who will accompany him or her out of the building, and so forth?		

Self-Assessment on Managing a Dismissal

Use this tool to reflect upon how you managed a dismissal situation. It can help you recognize what you did well and what perhaps you can do better the next time.

For each statement below, indicate on a scale of 1 to 5 how strongly you agree or disagree with the statement. A "1" means "strongly disagree"; a "5" means "strongly agree."

Statement	Rating				
	Low				High
	1	2	3	4	5
I received company information on policies and procedures.					
I requested coaching from human resources or others as needed on how to manage dismissing an employee.					
I sought legal counsel to make sure that I was handling the situation correctly and avoided a wrongful-dismissal suit.					
I oversaw the administrative details efficiently, including the completion of necessary paperwork.					
I reviewed the employee's files so I was up to date and informed about the situation.					
I kept a respectful, realistic attitude in communications with the employee.					
I acknowledged and dealt with my own emotions associated with dismissing an employee.					
I set up a private meeting with the employee and made arrangements so that meeting date was the employee's last day on the job.					
I made sure a human resource manager was present at the meeting to provide support and answer employee questions about the impact of the dismissal.					
I kept the meeting as short as possible, under ten minutes if possible.					
I maintained a dispassionate attitude and was direct, focused, and resolute.					
I delivered the news in a way that preserved the employee's dignity, and tried to strike a balance between being concise and empathetic.					
I cited reasons for the dismissal in a neutral tone as simply and directly as possible.					
I didn't get into details that might complicate the situation.					
I escorted or had a company representative escort the employee from the building.					

Other (fill in)

Test Yourself

This section offers ten multiple-choice questions to help you identify your baseline knowledge of dismissal essentials. Answers to the questions are given at the end of the test.

1. To dismiss an employee is to:

    a. Terminate an individual's employment with a company owing to inadequacies or problems with his or her performance or behavior.

    b. Terminate an individual's employment with a company owing to the firm's desire to take a new strategic direction or cut costs.

    c. Terminate an individual's employment with the company owing to the fact that the worker and his or her manager do not get along on a personal level.

2. Which of the following statements would *not* be appropriate to make when explaining to your team why someone was dismissed?

    a. Julia was dismissed because she was chronically late and abused sick leave privileges.

    b. Max was dismissed after many months of unsuccessful attempts to improve his performance.

    c. Trevor was dismissed because he falsified expense reports and could no longer be trusted.

3. Putting a problem employee on probation means:

a. Putting the employee on a paid or unpaid leave from work, during which he or she must create a plan for addressing the problem performance or behavior, clarify expectations, and establish new goals.

b. Temporarily suspending certain workplace benefits (such as flextime or the opportunity to work from home) until the employee can demonstrate that he or she has corrected his or her problem performance or behavior.

c. Issuing an oral and written warning to the employee in which you set a date by which he or she must improve the problem performance or behavior; the warning then gets documented and stored in the employee's personnel file.

4. True or false: You must provide a reference for a dismissed employee if he or she (or if a potential new employer) asks for one.

a. True.

b. False.

5. Which of the following statements would *not* be appropriate to make when dismissing an employee?

a. "The job hasn't worked out. You've continued to have unexcused absences over the past several months."

b. "The job hasn't worked out. We set new sales goals for you six months ago, and you still haven't met them."

c. "The job just has not worked out. We need someone who can project a high-energy, up-and-coming image."

6. In many companies, which of the following employee behaviors might constitute grounds for immediate dismissal?

a. An employee arrives at the office late several times in one week.

b. An employee steals a computer from his or her department.

c. An employee gossips with other workers on several occasions in one week.

7. There are certain employee behaviors for which a manager cannot legally dismiss the worker. Which of the following behaviors does *not* fall into that category?

a. The employee has taken time off from work to vote.

b. The employee has filed several workers' compensation claims.

c. The employee makes unwelcome, repeated sexual jokes during team meetings.

8. When you have to dismiss an employee, it's best to break the news to him or her in a private setting. Of the statements listed below, which of the following constitutes the most important reason for conducting the meeting in private?

a. If other employees see or hear what's happening, they may worry that they're next in line to be dismissed.

b. If other employees see or hear what's happening, they may criticize the dismissed employee afterward, worsening his or her pain.

c. If other employees see or hear what's happening, they may immediately protest the decision if they consider the dismissed employee their friend.

9. If you have to dismiss someone, when should you deliver the news to the person?

    a. As late in the work day as possible on a Friday afternoon.

    b. As early in the day as possible during the middle of the workweek.

    c. In the afternoon on a Monday.

10. Which of the following do *not* constitute important parts of leading your team after a dismissal?

    a. Reassuring remaining team members that the dismissal had nothing to do with their own performance as individuals or as a team.

    b. Celebrating the fact that the team can now function more smoothly because the problem worker has been removed.

    c. Ensuring that the former employee's skills are represented in the group and that his or her work is redistributed fairly among remaining team members.

Answers to test questions

1, a. An employee may be dismissed for problematic *performance*, such as failing to meet sales goals or consistently botching client presentations, or problematic *behavior*—for example, chronic lateness or constant blaming of others for the team's or company's problems.

2, c. This statement is *not* appropriate, because it contains a judgment about the employee's reputation ("Trevor could no longer be trusted"). Once an employee has been dismissed, you need to avoid doing or saying anything about that person that could be perceived as damaging to his or her reputation. Uttering damaging statements can potentially lead to defamation charges being brought against your company.

3, b. Probation is one of many alternatives to a dismissal and is worth considering if the problem employee has valued qualities or skills, or shows promise. Other dismissal alternatives include training, counseling, coaching, suspension, demotion, warning, and delaying of pay raises or bonuses.

4, b. You aren't legally bound to provide a reference for an employee you dismissed. However, by refusing to provide one, you may risk charges of blacklisting from the former employee. That's why many companies provide just factual information (dates of employment, job title, and final salary) when asked for such a reference.

5, c. This statement is *not* appropriate; it could imply that you dismissed the employee because he or she is too old. Dismissal on the basis of age or other personal characteristics such as gender, race, ethnic origins, marital status, religion, and so forth constitutes discrimination in many workplaces. And an employee who has been discriminated against is likely to be able to successfully sue your company for wrongful dismissal.

6, b. Stealing, threatening other workers, possessing an unapproved weapon at work, and other equally serious behaviors may constitute grounds for immediate dismissal. Be sure to consult legal counsel to make sure you understand the laws and regulations unique to your situation.

7, c. Sexually oriented references *can* constitute grounds for legal firing. Therefore, this employee behavior does not fall into the category of actions for which a manager can never dismiss the worker.

8, a. Of the reasons listed, the most important for conducting a dismissal meeting in private is to prevent a "siege mentality" from taking shape among the affected employee's coworkers. That is, coworkers who witness or overhear the meeting may conclude that they're just one mishap away from being dismissed themselves. And a siege mentality can erode morale and productivity.

9, c. Breaking the news of a dismissal to the affected employee on a Monday afternoon enables the person to begin looking for another job as quickly as possible—and to have the entire workweek to organize his or her job search.

10, b. Celebrating the loss of a problem employee is *not* an appropriate or important part of leading your team after a dismissal. A dismissal is painful for everyone involved, including the employee's manager and former coworkers. Thus it is never a cause for celebration.

Frequently Asked Questions

What documentation am I required to give the dismissed employee?

Consult legal counsel to confirm what documentation you should provide. In general, documentation should be as brief as possible but may include details of continued benefits, severance, effective dates of termination and pay, and, possibly, a nondisclosure or noncompete agreement. The documentation should not contain explanations of the reasons for the dismissal.

If I have to dismiss someone, can I get someone else to deliver the news, or can I do it by e-mail?

The short answer is, delivering this type of message, in person, is part of your job. As painful as delivering hard news is, it's much better to do it yourself, and in person. That's because people form relationships with their managers much more so than with their companies. By delivering hard news in person, you honor that relationship and the other person's humanity, and you help him or her achieve closure on the relationship. With closure, people find it much easier to move on.

Should I explain the rationale behind a dismissal?

A dismissal should never come as a surprise to the affected employee. If it does, the manager involved has not sufficiently communicated job expectations and performance feedback to the worker. If the employee wants to know why you're dismissing him or her, it's appropriate to say something like, "Here's the goal we agreed on six months ago. We discussed ways you would try to reach that goal. But you have not performed as we agreed." By providing a brief, honest response, you help the person achieve closure.

After dismissing someone, how quickly should I focus that person's attention on the future?

When people are dismissed, they often need time to process their emotions. When you deliver the news, give the affected employee time to vent and then to pull him- or herself together emotionally. Then direct his or her attention to the next steps. For some individuals, a difficult conversation is as much about feelings as it is about what's happening. If you ignore the person's emotions, you'll make it that much more difficult for the individual to get closure on the situation and move on. So, let people express themselves, but don't get drawn into debating the merits of your decision.

With a dismissal, should I usher people out immediately after their exit interview, or should I give them time to say good-bye to coworkers?

It's most appropriate to escort the person out of the building as soon as possible after termination of his or her employment with the company. He or she may return later for the scheduled exit interview.

What should I do about e-mail and phone messages for employees who have been dismissed?

If you're going to cancel the affected employee's e-mail accounts and voice mail immediately after a dismissal, make arrangements to forward any incoming messages to the employee for a designated amount of time.

Of course, with dismissed employees, you don't want suppliers or customers maintaining contact with a possibly bitter or vindictive former worker. On the other hand, it can be upsetting to these outside constituencies to be unable to reach a person they're used to working with—and to get no explanation from your company for what has happened.

Clearly, you need to make careful decisions regarding what kinds of communication channels you want to keep open, for how long, and in what respect. Balance concerns about what an abrupt communication cutoff may do to the company against any risks involved in forwarding messages to former workers for a time.

Your organization may have policies in place regarding these questions, so be sure to check with your supervisor or human resource department to make sure you're following those regulations.

It seems that managers can't say anything anymore without risking a lawsuit. What *can* I legally say during a dismissal meeting without prompting legal repercussions from the affected employee?

Employment laws vary widely from state to state, country to country, and even employee to employee (in the sense of laws governing employment of unionized versus nonunionized workers or exempt versus nonexempt workers). Thus you must consult your organization's legal department to ensure that you're handling a dismissal meeting correctly. Some rules of thumb may help—for example, it's generally safer legally to keep your comments as concise and neutral as possible. However, do check with your company's legal counsel to make sure you understand—and follow—the law and your firm's policies.

Key Terms

Blacklisting. Preventing a former employee from finding another job by making critical or defamatory statements about him or her to potential employers who call for a reference.

Demotion. Moving a problem performer to a role that requires fewer skills and that pays less, to create a better match between the person and the job.

Discrimination. Dismissing an employee on the basis of his or her race, sex, age, marital status, sexual orientation, reproductive status (whether an employee is pregnant or plans to become pregnant), physical or mental disability, ethnic background, and other distinguishing characteristics that fall under the protection of federal or state law or company policy.

Dismissal. The termination of an individual's employment with a company owing to inadequacies or problems with his or her performance or behavior.

Exempt employees. Salaried workers who are exempt from being paid overtime; companies and federal and state laws distinguish between exempt and nonexempt employees in determining dismissal policies.

Exit interview. A meeting during which a dismissed employee candidly shares his or her concerns or complaints with a human resource staff member; can be used to identify areas for improvement within the company.

Noncompete agreement. A contract by which a former employee agrees not to work for a competing company for a specific period of time after leaving his or her current firm.

Nondisclosure agreement. A contract by which a former employee agrees not to use sensitive information (such as trade secrets or stock information) to his or her advantage after leaving the current employer.

Nonexempt employees. Hourly workers who may be paid overtime; companies and federal and state laws distinguish between exempt and nonexempt employees in determining dismissal policies.

Probation. Temporary suspension of workplace privileges (such as flextime or the ability to work from home) for a problem employee; during the probation period, the employee is expected to work on improving his or her performance or behavior.

Severance. A package consisting of pay and possibly benefits extended to dismissed employees to ease their financial hardship or to gain their agreement not to sue the company for wrongful dismissal.

Support network. The family, friends, colleagues, and helping professionals who can assist managers in navigating through a dismissal; support-network members help by listening and by offering advice and moral support.

Suspension. A temporary paid or unpaid leave for a problem employee during which the person is expected to formulate new goals.

Termination. A synonym for *dismissal*.

Wrongful-dismissal suit. A lawsuit in which a dismissed employee claims that he or she was illegally let go by his or her former employer.

To Learn More

Articles

Peace, William H. "The Hard Work of Being a Soft Manager." *Harvard Business Review* OnPoint Enhanced Edition (2001).

> Soft management does not mean weak management, says William Peace in this 1991 article. It means candor, openness, and vulnerability, but it also means hard choices and responsible follow-up. It means taking the heat for difficult decisions and giving unhappy subordinates chances to unburden themselves at your expense.

Weeks, Holly. "Taking the Stress Out of Stressful Conversations." *Harvard Business Review* OnPoint Enhanced Edition (March 2002).

> Dismissing an employee can be one of the most stressful conversations a manager can face. That's because such conversations are emotionally loaded. Weeks explains the emotional dynamics that take place in stressful conversations and emphasizes the importance of preparation before delivering painful news to an employee. She describes a method for identifying your vulnerabilities during stressful conversations and practicing more effective delivery styles and behaviors.

Books

Delpo, Amy, and Lisa Guerin. *Dealing with Problem Employees: A Legal Guide.* Berkeley, CA: Nolo, 2001.

> Problem employees pose an enormous number of legal and other challenges. This book shows you how to recognize who is and isn't a problem employee, help problem employees get back on track, investigate problems and complaints, conduct effective performance evaluations, apply progressive discipline, and handle the many complex aspects of dismissals.

Repa, Barbara Kate. *Firing Without Fear: A Legal Guide for Conscientious Employers.* Berkeley, CA: Nolo, 2000.

> Myths about the right way to dismiss a problem worker abound. This concise resource tells you everything you need to know about intervention and retraining; the process for deciding whether to dismiss an employee; the nuts and bolts of delivering the painful news; and the laws, myths, and realities surrounding firing. As the authors make clear, you need to take important steps before, during, and after dismissing someone to reduce the risks of a wrongful-dismissal lawsuit. This book shows you how.

Stone, Douglas, Bruce Patton, and Sheila Heen. *Difficult Conversations: How to Discuss What Matters Most.* New York: Penguin Books, 1999.

> Informing an employee that he or she is being dismissed counts among the most difficult conversations a manager can face. This book explains how to keep a cool head in a wide

range of difficult conversations—not only in the workplace but also in the other important areas of your life. The principles and practices described here can benefit you no matter what kind of difficult conversation you're facing.

eLearning Programs

Harvard Business School Publishing. *Managing Direct Reports.* Boston: Harvard Business School Publishing, 2000.

Learn the skills and concepts you need to effectively manage direct reports and be able to apply these techniques immediately to your own situation. Through interactive practice scenarios, expert guidance, on-the-job activities, and a mentoring feature, you will learn and practice how to:

- Understand direct reports' expectations
- Manage a network of relationships
- Delegate along a continuum

Pre- and post-assessments and additional resources complete the workshop, preparing you for more productive direct report relationships.

Sources for Dimissing an Employee

We would like to acknowledge the sources who aided in developing this topic.

Delpo, Amy, and Lisa Guerin. *Dealing with Problem Employees: A Legal Guide.* Berkeley, CA: Nolo, 2001.

Gosset, Steve. "Sometimes You Do Have to Fire People: Making Sure the End Is Not Really the Beginning of More Headaches." *Harvard Management Communication Letter* (October 1999).

Morgan, Nick. "The Three Toughest Presentations." *Harvard Management Communication Letter* (September 2001).

Repa, Barbara Kate. *Firing Without Fear: A Legal Guide for Conscientious Employers.* Berkeley, CA: Nolo, 2000.

Weeks, Holly. "Taking the Stress Out of Stressful Conversations." *Harvard Business Review* OnPoint Enhanced Edition (2002).